PIANO • VOCAL • CHORDS

THE ROLLING S

LET IT BLEED

ALBUM NOTES

Release Date: December 5, 1969
Top Chart Position: No. 3, reached December 20, 1969
Standout Tracks: "Midnight Rambler," "Gimme Shelter," "You Can't Always Get What You Want" and "Let It Bleed"
Significance: Recorded mostly without founding member and original lead guitarist, Brian Jones—who left the band before the album was finished; released at roughly the same time as the band's infamous free concert in Altamont, California; introduced American Mick Taylor as the new guitarist.
Milestone: Featured Keith Richards' first lead vocal performance with the song "You Got the Silver"; when the album reached No. 1 in the U.K., it displaced the Beatles' Abbey Road.

Alfred Publishing Co., Inc.
16320 Roscoe Blvd., Suite 100
P.O. Box 10003
Van Nuys, CA 91410-0003
alfred.com

In Association with ABKCO Music Inc.
1700 Broadway
New York, New York 10019
abkco.com

Exclusively distributed by Alfred Publishing.

ISBN-10: 0-7390-4148-7
ISBN-13: 978-0-7390-4148-2

FOREWORD

The last Rolling Stones album of the 1960s, Let It Bleed, was released on December 5, 1969, timed to coincide with the band's first U.S. tour in three years. December 6th would find them playing the infamous free concert at Altamont, California, documented in Albert and David Maysles' film Gimme Shelter—which derived its title from the first track on the U.K. release of the album. Sadly, the foreboding, apocalyptic vision of the song was born out by the mayhem of that night. "Midnight Rambler" is also thematically frightening as it invokes the Boston Strangler, who had, only two years earlier, been convicted of murdering 13 women. Clearly, the decade was ending on a dark note and the Stones were providing the soundtrack.

Though Brian Jones contributed percussion and autoharp to "Midnight Rambler" and "You Got the Silver," he officially departed the band on June 9th of that year. Two weeks before his death on July 3rd, he was replaced by Mick Taylor, a 21-year-old American who had played in John Mayall's Bluesbreakers. Taylor made his performance debut with the band at a huge free concert in London's Hyde Park that took place two days after Jones's death. Like the man he replaced, Taylor is heard on only two tracks of Let It Bleed: "Country Honk," a countrified version of the hit single "Honky Tonk Women," and "Live with Me."

Produced by Jimmy Miller, who had worked on Beggars Banquet, the album presents a broad spectrum of stylistic diversity. Guest musicians include former Raelette Mary Clayton, whose searing vocals are heard on "Gimme Shelter;" keyboard men Nicky Hopkins, Ian Stewart and Leon Russell; Ry Cooder (mandolin); Al Kooper (keyboards and French horn); Bobby Keys (sax); and Byron Berline (fiddle), among others. "You Can't Always Get What You Want" features the London Bach Choir augmented by a female soul gospel chorus including Madelaine Bell, Doris Troy and Nanette Newman, with percussion by Rocky Dijon and a brilliant arrangement by Jack Nitzche. The track is thought to be the Stones' counterpoint to the Beatles' "Hey Jude." (Of course, the album's title is clearly a clever riposte to Let It Be.) Along these same lines, it should be noted that Let It Bleed climbed to No. 1 on the U.K. album charts, displacing Abbey Road from the top slot.

Save for the mesmerizing version of Robert Johnson's blues classic "Love in Vain," all of the songs were Jagger-Richards compositions with Keith Richards' first-ever lead vocal heard on the plaintive "You Got the Silver."

Let It Bleed is acknowledged today as one of the most powerful of all Rolling Stones albums. Recorded and released during a time of turmoil in the world and within the band, these songs endure as testimony to the power of the Stones' transcendent artistry. Despite or, perhaps, because of the bleak vision of most of these songs, they have endured through the years like the Stones themselves.

CONTENTS

LET IT BLEED

Words and Music by
MICK JAGGER and KEITH RICHARDS

D
F
Yeah, we all need some - one we can lean on.
Yeah, we all need some - one we can cream on.
D7
F7
E7
G7
A
C
To Coda
And if you want it, well, you can lean on me.
And if you want to, well, you can cream on me.
Verse 1:
C♯7
E7
D
F
1. She said, "My breasts, they will al - ways be o - pen.
E7
G7
A
C
Ba - by, you can rest your wear - y head right on me.

C#7
E7
And there will al - ways be a space in my park -
D
F
E7
G7
ing lot when you need a lit - tle
D.S. 𝄋 al Coda
coke and sym - pa - thy." 2. Yeah, we all
Coda
Verse 2:
A
C
C#7
E7
2. I was dream - ing of a steel gui - tar en - gage -

D7
F7
E7
G7
ment_ when you drunk my health_ in scen - ted jas - mine tea.
A
C
C#7
E7
But_ you knifed_ me in_ my dirt - y, filth - y base-
D7
F7
E7
G7
ment_ with that jad - ed, fad - ed, junk - y nurse. Oh,_ what plea-
Chorus 3:
A7
C7
sant com-pan - y,_ hah! 3. Don't_ we all_ need some - one we can feed_

D
F
D7
F7
E7
G7
on.
Yeah, and if you want it,
well, you can feed on me.
A7
C7
Hey!
Take my arm,
take my leg,
D7
F7
E7
G7
oh, ba - by, don't you take my head.
A
C
Chorus 4:
A7
C7
Whoo!
4. Yeah, we all need some - one we can

D
F
D7
F7
E7
G7
bleed on.__
Yeah,_ and if you want it, ba - by, well, you can bleed on me._
A
C
A7
C7
Yeah!____
We all____ need some - one we can bleed_
D
F
E7
G7
__ on.__
Yeah, yeah,_ and if you want it, ba - by, why don't - cha bleed__ on me_
A7
C7
__ all o - ver.
Whoo!
(Inst. solo ad lib.…

D7
F7
E7
G7
A
C
1.
2.
A7
C7
Ahh,
...end solo)
get it on, rid - er,
whoo!
Get it on, rid - er,
get it on, rid - er,
Repeat ad lib. and fade
you can bleed all o - ver me,
yeah!

LOVE IN VAIN

Words and Music by
ROBERT JOHNSON

G
D
G
Gsus
G
B♭
F
B♭
B♭sus
B♭
Whoa,_ it's
D
D/F♯
Em7
C
F
F/A
Gm7
E♭
hard to tell, it's hard to tell
when all your love's_____ in
G
G7
D
B♭
B♭7
F
vain.
2. When the
…end solo)
4. When the
Verses 2 & 4:
G
B♭
train_____ come in the sta - tion,_
train_____ left the sta - tion,_

G7
B♭7
I looked her in the eye.
it had two lights on be-hind.
Well, the
When the
C
E♭
D7/F#
F7/A
train come in the sta - tion
train left the sta - tion,
and I looked her in the eye.
it had two lights on be - hind.
G
B♭
D
F
G
B♭
Gsus
B♭sus
G
B♭
Whoa, I
Whoa, the
D
F
Em7
Gm7
C
E♭
felt so sad, so lone - some
blue light was my ba - by,
that I could not help but
and the red light was my

G
G7
1. D
2. D
B♭
B♭7
F
F
cry.
mind.
(Inst. solo ad lib....
C
E♭
D7/F♯
F7/A
Gsus
B♭sus
...end solo)
Em
Gm
All my love's in vain.
rit.

MIDNIGHT RAMBLER

Words and Music by
MICK JAGGER and
KEITH RICHARDS

E5
B5
A5
E5
Did you hear a - bout the mid - night ram - bler? The
A - talk - in' 'bout the mid - night gam - bler, did you
B5
A5
E5
Verses 1 & 2:
A5
E5
one that shut the kit - chen door? 1. He don't give you a hoot out of warn -
see him jump the gar - den wall? 2. Sigh - in' down the wind so sad -
B5
A5
E5
B5
ing, wrapped up in a black cat cloak. He
ly, lis - ten and you'll hear him moan. Yeah, well,
A5
E5
B5
A5
E5
don't go in the light of the morn - ing, he split the time the cock will crow.
talk - in' 'bout the mid - night gam - bler, ev - 'ry - bod - y got to go.

1.
B5
2.
B5
2. I'm
Interlude:
B5
A5
E5
B5
A5
E5
(2nd time inst. solo ad lib....
B5
A5
E5
B5
A5
1.
E5

2.
Verse 3:
E5
A5
E5
B5
...end solo) 3. Did you hear a - bout__ the mid-night ram - bler? Well, hon -
A5
E5
B5
A5
E5
ey, it's no rock 'n' roll show.__ Well, I'm a - talk - in' 'bout the mid-night gam -
B5
A5
E5
B5
bler, yeah, the one you nev - er seen be - fore.
Instrumental:
B5
1.
(2nd time inst. solo ad lib....

2.
accel. poco a poco & straighten 8ths
Driving rock feel ♩=152
B5
(Cont. solo, with vocal ad lib.)
Oh, don't do that. Oh, don't do that. Yeah, oh, don't do
that. Yeah, don't you dare do that. Don't you dare do that. Don't do that.

B5
1.-6.
(Cont. solo, with vocal ad lib.)
7.
...end solo) Don't do that. Oh, don't do that. Oh, don't do
that. Oh, don't do that. Oh, don't do that. Oh, don't do
(Drums stop)
that.
(Laughter)

Very slow & rubato ♩ = 50
(Play 3 times)
Chorus 3:
B5
A5
4. Well, you heard a - bout the Bos - ton...
E5
B5
A5
E5
It's not one of those.
Well,
B5
A5
E5
B5
A5
talk - in' 'bout the mid - night...
unh! shh!
The one that closed the bed - room door.

Verse 4:
E5
A5
E5
B5
4. I'm called the hit-and-run rap-er in an-ger, The
A5
E5
B5
A5
E5
knife-shar-pened tip-pie-toe.... Or just the shoot 'em dead, brain-bell jang-
B5
A5
E5
B5
ler, you know, the one you nev-er seen be-fore. 5. So, if you
Verse 5:
A5
E5
B5
ev-er meet the mid-night ram-bler a-
(A little faster)

A5
E5
B5
coming down your marble hall, well, he's
(Drums re-enter full)
A5
E5
B5
pouncing like a proud black panther. Well, you can
A5
E5
B5
say I, I told you so! 6. Well, don't-cha
Verse 6:
A5
E5
B5
listen for the midnight rambler, hey, yah, play it
(A little faster)

A5
E5
B5
easy as you go.
I'm gonna
Straight 8ths
smash down all your plate glass windows, put a fist, put a
fist through your steel-plated door!
accel. poco a poco
(Harmonica solo ad lib.)

4. Did you
Tempo I (♩ = 126)
Chorus 4:
B5
A5
E5
7
5
hear a-bout the mid-night ram - bler?
He'll leave his foot-prints up and down_ your hall._
And did you hear__ a-bout_ the mid-night gam - bler?
And did you see_

Verse 7:
B5
A5
E5
A5
E5
me make my mid-night call?
7. And if you ev - er catch the mid-night ram-
B5
A5
E5
B5
bler, I'll steal your mis - tress from un - der your nose. I'll go eas-
A5
E5
B5
y with your cold fanged an - ger. I'll stick my
A5
E5
knife right down your throat, ba - by, and it hurts!

GIMME SHELTER

Words and Music by
MICK JAGGER and KEITH RICHARDS

Optional Guitar in Open G tuning:
⑥ = D ③ = G
⑤ = G ② = B
④ = D ① = D

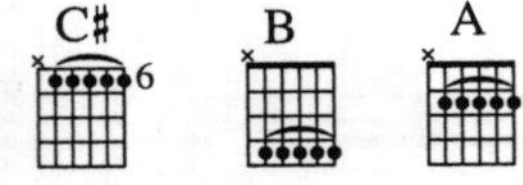

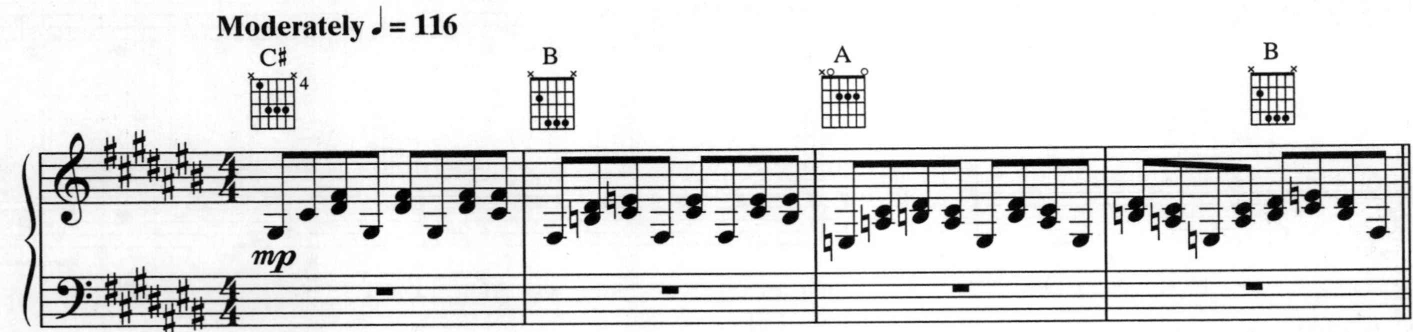

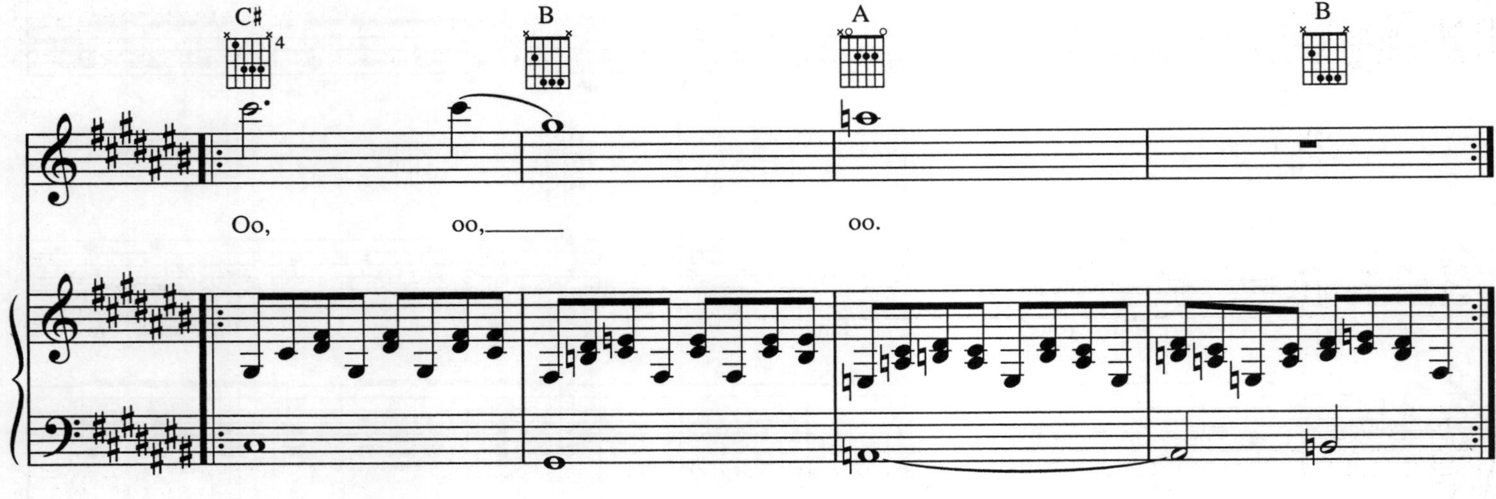

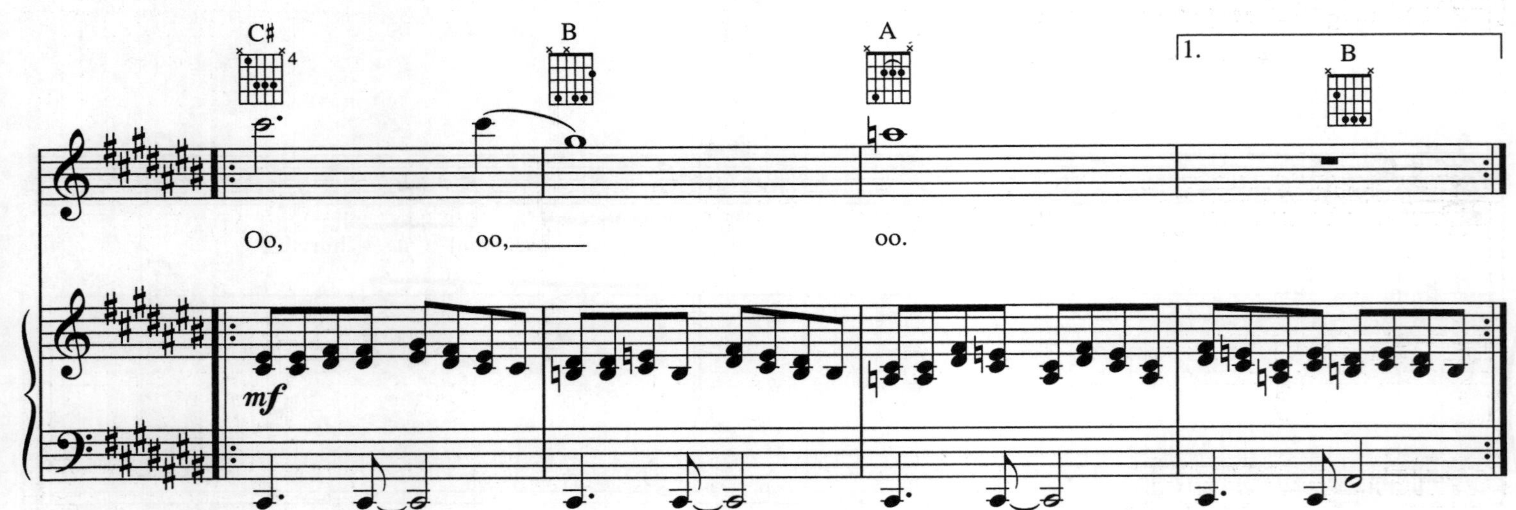

2.

C♯ B

A

E A E A E B E B

Verse:

C♯

1. Oo, a storm is threat - 'ning my very - y life today.
2. Ooh, see the fire is sweep - in' our ver - y street today.
3. Mm, the flood is threat - 'ning my ver - y life today.

If I don't get some shel - ter,
Burns like a red coat car - pet;
Gim - me, gim - me shel - ter

To Coda ⊕

ooh yeah, I'm gon - na fade a - way.
mad bull lost your way.
or I'm gon - na
Chorus:
C♯
B
A
War, chil - dren, it's just a shot a - way,
E A E A E B E B C♯
it's just a shot a - way. War, chil -
B
A
E A E A E B E B
dren, it's just a shot a - way, it's just a shot a - way.

C♯
(Inst. solo ad lib....
1.
2.
C♯
B
A

1.2.
E A E A E B E B
3.
E A E A E B E B
…end solo)
Chorus:
C♯ B A
Rape, mur - der! It's just a shot a - way,
E A E A E B E B C♯
It's just a shot a - way. Rape,
B A
mur - der, yeah! It's just a shot a - way,

E A E A E B E B C♯ B
It's just a shot a - way.
Rape,
mur - der!
A E A E A E B E B C♯
It's just a shot a-way,
It's just a shot a - way,
yeah, yeah,
D.S. 𝄋 al Coda
yeah.
𝄌 Coda
Chorus:
C♯ B
fade a - way.
War,
chil - dren,

A
E
A
E
A
E
B
E
B
it's just a shot a - way,
it's just a shot a - way.
C#
4
B
A
It's just a shot a - way,
it's just a shot a - way,
it's just a shot a - way.
E
A
E
A
E
B
E
B
C#
4
I tell you love,
B
A
sis - ter,
it's just a kiss a - way,

E A E A E B E B C♯

it's just a kiss a - way.___ It's just a kiss a - way,___

B A

it's just a kiss a - way,___ it's just a kiss a - way,

E A E A E B E B C♯ B

kiss a - way, kiss a - way.___

Repeat ad lib. and fade

A E A E A E B E B

YOU GOT THE SILVER

Guitar in Open E tuning:
⑥ = E ③ = G♯
⑤ = B ② = B
④ = E ① = E

Words and Music by
MICK JAGGER and KEITH RICHARDS

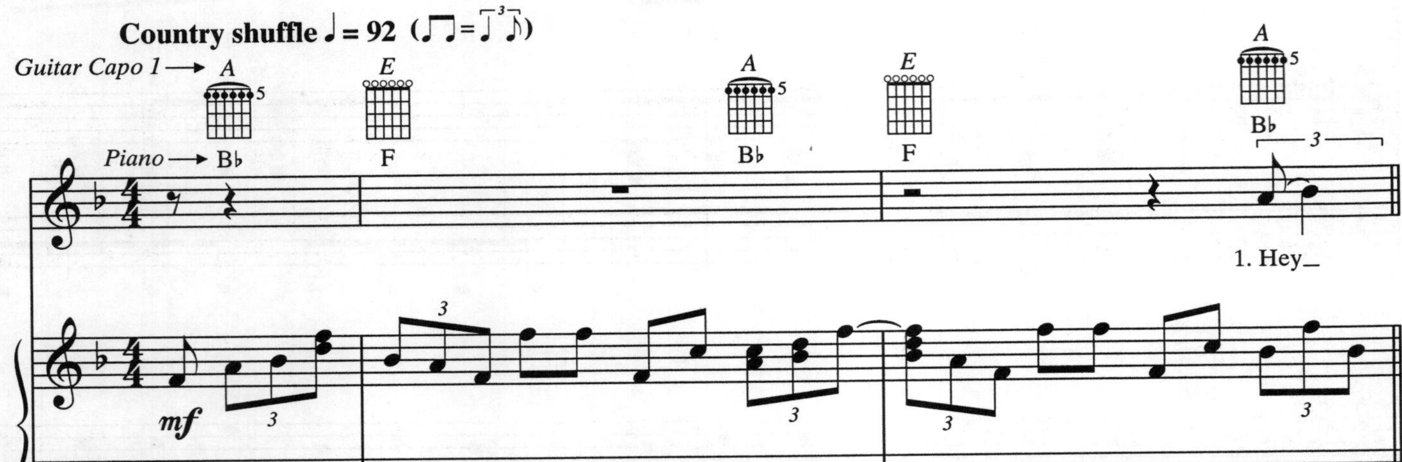

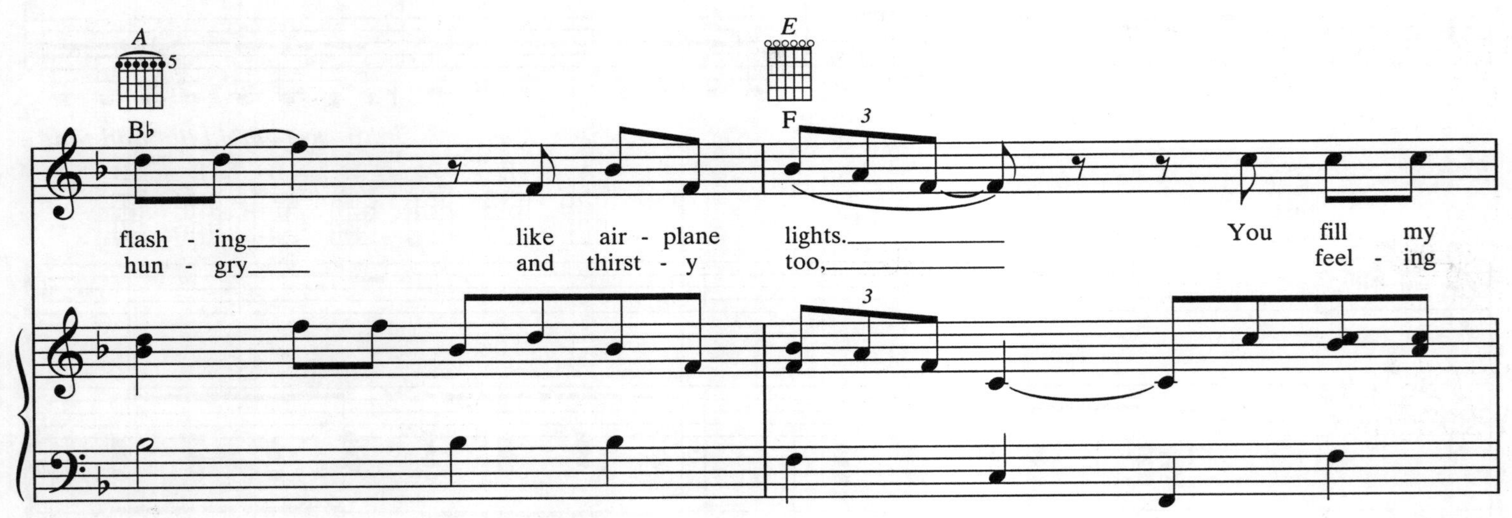

A
E
A
B♭
F
B♭
cup, babe,_ that's for sure._ Must come back
fool - ish,_ and that's for sure,_ just wait-ing here
N.C.
To Coda
for a lit - tle more.
at your kitch - en door?
You got my
Chorus:
E
A
F
B♭
heart,_ you got my soul._ You got the sil - ver,_ you got the
A
E
B♭
F
gold._ You got the dia - monds_ from the mine._ Well, that's al -

A2
B♭2
A
B♭
B
C N.C.
right,
it-'ll buy some time.
Instrumental:
E
F
A
B♭
E
F
A
B♭
E
F
A
B♭
B
C N.C.
D.S. 𝄋 al Coda
2. Tell me,

Coda

Bridge:

E
F

Hey ba - by, what's in your

A
B♭
E
F

eyes? Is that the dia - monds from the mine? What's that

A
B♭
E
F
A
B♭

laugh - ing in your smile? I don't care, no,

B
C N.C.

I don't care. Oh

Chorus:

E
A
F
F
B♭
babe, you got my soul. You got the sil - ver, you got the
E
A
E
F
B♭
F
gold. It's just your love, just leave me blind. I don't
A
B
B♭
C
care, no, that's no big sur - prise.
E
F
rit.

YOU CAN'T ALWAYS GET WHAT YOU WANT

Guitar in Open E tuning *(optional w/ Capo at 8th fret)*:
⑥ = E ③ = G♯
⑤ = B ② = B
④ = E ① = E

Words and Music by
MICK JAGGER and
KEITH RICHARDS

Moderately ♩ = 104

want.__ You can't al - ways get what you want.__ And if you
aah. Aah, aah,
try some time__ you'll find__ you get what you need.
aah, aah, aah.
(Guitar)
mp
F
C
C2
C
C2
C
C2
C
C2
C
F
(French Horn)
C2
* (Cont. chord pattern throughout)
F
C2

F
C2
F
(Lead Vocal) 1. I
Verses 1 & 5:
C2
F
saw her to - day at the re - cep - tion,
5. See additional lyrics
C2
F
a glass of wine in her hand.
I knew
C2
F
she was gon - na meet her con - nec - tion.
At her

C2
F
feet was a foot - loose man.
You
Chorus:
C2
F
can't al - ways get what you want.
You
C2
F
can't al - ways get what you want.
You
C2
F
To Coda
can't al - ways get what you want.
But if you

D
F
C7
try some - times,
well, you might
find
you get what you
need.
Oh,
F
C7
F
yeah.
2. And I went
Verses 2, 3, & 4:
C2
F
down
to the
dem - on
-
stra
-
tion
to get
3. 4. See additional lyrics
C2
F
my
fair
share
of
a
-
buse.
Sing - in', "We're

C2
F
gon - na vent our frus - tra - tion.
If we don't,
1. 3.
To Next Strain
we're gon - na blow a fif - ty - amp fuse."
Sing it to me, now.
You
2.
Chorus:
C7
4. We de - cid - can't al - ways get what you want.
F7
You can't al - ways get what you want.

F7
C7
F7
You can't al - ways get what you want.
But if you
D
F
try some - times,
well, you just might find,
you get what you
1.
C7
F7
C7
need.
Oh
ba - by, yeah.
F7
2.
C7
F7
3. I
need.
Oh,
yeah.
Whoo!

D7sus/A
D7sus/B
D7sus/C
(Choir)
Aah,
aah,
D7sus
D7sus/G
aah,
aah.
Chorus:
C7
F7
C7
Aah,
aah,
aah,
F7
C7
F7
aah,
aah,
aah.

D
F
C7
You get what you need.
F7
C7
F7
D.S. 𝄋 al Coda
5. I
Coda
D
F
try some - time, you just might find, you just might find you get what you
C7
F7
need.
aah,
(Choir) Aah,

Verse 3:
I went down to the Chelsea drugstore
To get your prescription filled.
I was standin' in line with Mr. Jimmy.
A-man, did he look pretty ill.

Verse 4:
We decided that we would have a soda;
My favorite flavor, cherry red,
I sung my song to Mr. Jimmy.
Yeah, and he said one word to me, and that was "dead."
I said to him…
(To Chorus:)

Verse 5:
I saw her today at the reception.
In her glass was a bleeding man.
She was practiced at the art of deception.
Well, I could tell by her blood-stained hands.
Say it!
(To Chorus:)

LIVE WITH ME

Words and Music by
MICK JAGGER and KEITH RICHARDS

Moderately fast, driving rock ♩ = 132

N.C.

mf

Verses 1, 2, & 3:

D

1. I got nasty habits, I take tea at three.___ Yes, and the meat I eat___ for dinner___ amust be hung up for a week._

score of hare-brained children, they're all a-locked in the nursery. They got earphone heads,_ they got dirty necks,_ they're so twentieth century.___

3. *(Inst. solo ad lib.…*

A D A D A D

A
D
A
My best friend, he shoots wa - ter rats and
Well, they queue up for the bath - room 'round a-bout
D
A
D
a - feeds them to his geese.
sev - en thir - ty - five.
Don't - cha think there's a
Don't - cha think we need a
A
D
A
place for you in be - tween the sheets?
wom - an's touch to make it come a - live?
1. Come
Chorus 1 & 2:
E
G
A
on now, hon-ey, we can build a home for cheap.
2. You'd look good pram push-ing down the high street.
3. (solo cont....

E
G
Come on now, hon-ey, don't you wan-na live with me?
1.
A
2.
A
2. And there's a
3.
A
...end solo) 4. Whoa, the
Verse 4:
D
A
D
ser-vants they're so help-ful, dear, the cook she is a whore.

A
D/A
5
A
Yes, the but-ler has a place for her be-
D/A
5
A
D/A
5
hind the pan - try door.
Whoo! The maid, she's French, she's
A
D/A
5
A
got no sense, she's found the Cra - zy Horse.
And
D/A
5
A
D/A
5
when she strips, the chauf-feur flips, the foot-man's eyes get crossed.

A D/A A

Whoo! Don't-cha think there's a place for us___

D/A A D/A

right a-cross the street?___ Don't-cha think there's a

A D/A A

place for you___ in be-tween the sheets?___

Repeat ad lib. and fade

D/A A D/A A

COUNTRY HONK

Words and Music by
MICK JAGGER and KEITH RICHARDS

G
C
many a bar-room queen I've had in Jackson,
but I just
G
D
G
can't seem to drink you off my mind.
It's the hon-
Chorus:
D
G
ky tonk wom-en.
D
G
Gim-me, gim-me, gim-me the hon-ky tonk blues.
2. I

Verses 2 & 3:

C
laid a di - vor - cée in New York Cit - y.
I
3. (Fiddle solo ad lib....
G
A7
D
had to put up some kind of a fight.
Whoo! The
G
C
la-dy she all dressed me up in ros - es.
She
G
D
G
blew my nose and then she blew my mind.
...end solo)
It's the hon-

Chorus:

D G

ky tonk_ wom-en.

D G 1.

Gim-me, gim-me, gim-me the hon-ky tonk_ blues._____

2. D G

It's the hon - ky tonk_ wom-en.

D G

Gim-me, gim-me, gim-me the hon-ky tonk_ blues._____

MONKEY MAN

Words and Music by
MICK JAGGER and
KEITH RICHARDS

(8va)
G/B
A/C♯
Bm
C♯m
Bm7
C♯m7
Bm6
C♯m6
G/B
A/C♯
B
C♯
1. I'm a
Verse 1:
D
E
flea - bit, pea - nut mon - key. All my friends are junk - ies.
B
C♯
That's not real - ly true. I'm a

D
E
cold I - tal - ian piz - za. I could use a lem - on squeez - er.
B
C♯
What you do?
1. But I've been
Chorus 1:
G
A
A
B
bit and I've been tossed a - round ev - 'ry she - rat in this town.
B
C♯
Have you, babe?
Well,

G
A
A
B
I am just a mon - key man an' I'm glad you are a mon - key
B
C♯
wom - an too.
2. I was
Verse 2:
D
E
bit - ten by a boar. I was gouged and I was gored
B
C♯
but I pulled on through.
Yes,

D
E
I'm a sack of bro - ken eggs. I al - ways have an un - made bed.
B
C♯
Don't you? 2. Well, I
Chorus 2:
G
A
A
B
hope we're not too mes - si - an - ic or a tri - fle too sa - tan - ic.
B
C♯
We love to play the blues. Well,

G 3 A 5

A B

I am just a mon - key man.__ I'm glad you are__ a mon - key,

B

C♯

mon - key wom-an too,__ babe!______

Interlude:

(Guitar solo ad lib….

...end solo)
Bridge:
D
E
A
B
G
A
A
B
D
E
(Piano solo ad lib....
A
B

1. 2.
3.
G
A
A
B
A
B
...end solo) I'm a
B
C♯
mon - key!
I'm a
mon - key!
(2nd time lead vocal ad lib.)
I'm a
(Bass tacet 1st time)
mon - key
man!
I'm a

mon - key
man!
I'm a
mon-key!
I'm a mon - key!
I'm a
(Lead vocal ad lib.)
Repeat ad lib. and fade